A special gift for

_____

with love,

_____

date

_____

For my three wonderful sons,
**Shannon, Travis,
and Kalen Morrow,**
who know their mom
will always be a kid at heart.

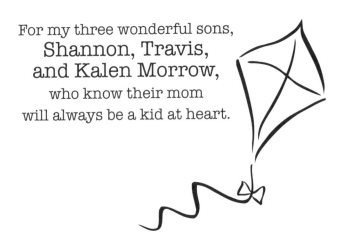

Other great books that take a little look at the big things of life:

Life's Too Short to Give Up Slumber Parties
—for Girlfriends

Life's Too Short to Look for Missing Socks
—for Moms

Life's Too Short to Yell at Your Computer
—for the Workplace

Available where good books are sold.

A Little Look at the Big Things of Life

Life's
Too Short

o Leave Kite Flying to Kids

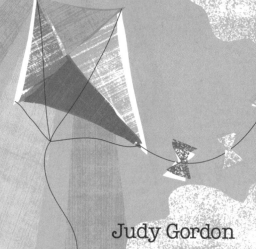

for Busy Grownups

Judy Gordon

Our purpose at Howard Publishing is to:
• *Increase faith* in the hearts of growing Christians
• *Inspire holiness* in the lives of believers
• *Instill hope* in the hearts of struggling people everywhere
Because He's coming again!

Life's Too Short to Leave Kite Flying to Kids © 2005 by Howard Publishing Co., Inc.
All rights reserved. Printed in China
Published by Howard Publishing Co., Inc.
3117 North 7th Street, West Monroe, LA 71291-2227
www.howardpublishing.com

05   06   07   08   09   10   11   12   13   14   10 9 8 7 6 5 4 3 2 1

Edited by Between the Lines and Chrys Howard
Cover design by LinDee Loveland
Interior design by Stephanie D. Walker and Tennille Paden
Illustrations by Cindy Sartain

ISBN: 1-58229-421-6

Unless otherwise noted, Scripture quotations are taken from the HOLY BIBLE, NEW INTERNATIONAL VERSION®. Copyright © 1973, 1978, 1984 by International Bible Society. Used by permission of Zondervan Publishing House. All rights reserved. Scriptures marked "The Message" are taken from *THE MESSAGE*. Copyright © 1993, 1994, 1995, 1996, 2000, 2001, 2002. Used by permission of NavPress Publishing Group.

Contents

Chapter
One

The Child
Inside

Life's
Too Short

to leave the
pleasures of childhood
to children.

for cartwheels

Life's
Too Short

to be left to kids.

the child inside

We've all heard the expression "There's a child in every adult." How true! Some of us are just better than others at inviting the child within to come out to play in our adult world.

How do you view life? With eyes half-closed or with the wide-open gaze of a child—receptive to adventure, imagination, and wonder? Do you feel a stirring of that child within you even now?

Freeing the kid in you balances you as a person. The playfulness of the child tempers the seriousness of the adult. The curiosity of that kid keeps your mind fresh and open to new ideas. Your youthful explorer spurs your more settled self to take risks and step up to new challenges.

Your inner child is calling you to live a life full of zest and adventure—a life of fun and hope and infinite possibilities. By the way, when *was* the last time you flew a kite?

Jesus called the children
to him and said,
"Let the little children come to me,
and do not hinder them,
for the kingdom of God
belongs to such as these."

LUKE 18:16

Life's
Too Short
to simply watch children play.

always

Life's
Too Short
for grownups to
always act like
grownups.

What do you miss most about being a kid?
What treat or activity
would put a smile on your face?
Go out and buy those Cracker Jacks.
Re-read your favorite children's book.
Skate!

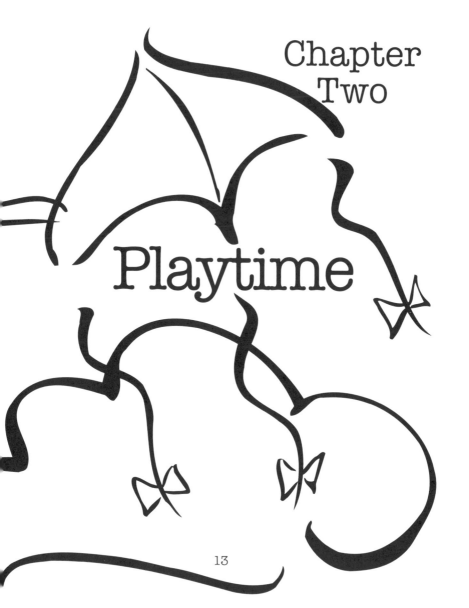

Chapter
Two

Playtime

Life's
Too Short to let winter

pass without

building a snowman.

snowman snowman snowman snowman snowman snowman snowman snowman snowman snowman snowman

Life's
Too Short

to let summer pass without

building a sandcastle.

playtime

Do you ever feel that you work too much and play too little? The old saying is true: "All work and no play makes Jack a dull boy" (or Jill a dull girl). Yet our adult lives overflow with work in every realm, and many of us feel guilty when we're not working. Too often we even measure our worth by how many things we've crossed off our To Do list by the end of the day. Maybe we've become too grown up for our own good.

Let the kid in you come out again. Some playtime will soften those deepening frown wrinkles and put a contented smile on your face. Think back to your favorite times of play as a child and give yourself permission to do those things again. Life is short. Take time to play.

Sing to him a new song;
play skillfully,
and shout for joy.

PSALM 33:3

climb

climb

it.

climb

to

to

afraid

too

be

but

tree

a

of

beauty

Life's

the

Too Short

enjoy

to

climb

to chew bubble gum

Life's
Too Short

without blowing a bubble.

See how high you can swing.
Fly down a slide with wax paper.
Play hide-and-seek and hopscotch.
Skip! You can't skip without feeling
like a child again. Try it and see!

Chapter Three

Simple Pleasures

Life's
Too Short

to r i n s e

the beaters
without licking them first.

licking them first

ice-cream truck

of an

to ignore the call

Life's
Too Short

simple pleasures

Have you ever found that the things you most hoped would bring pleasure often bring the greatest disappointment? Fortunately the opposite can also be true: the simplest of pleasures can bring the greatest enjoyment. Life is funny that way, isn't it?

A trip to Disneyland can yield expenses and exhaustion that outweigh the fun, while roasting marshmallows over a campfire can bring sweet sighs of contentment. A day of shopping at the mall can't compare with a day of relaxation at the beach. Remember how good the warm sand feels between your toes? Better than your feet feel after shopping, right?

What simple pleasures of your childhood brought you the most satisfaction? What put serenity in your soul and a lilt in your voice? Life is too short to refrain from enjoying those simple pleasures today.

The cheerful heart
has a continual feast.

PROVERBS 15:15

Life's
Too Short

to hide under

an umbrella

during a
summer
shower.

holding hands

Life's
Too Short

to walk

side by side

without holding hands.

When's the last time you treated yourself
to a root-beer float
or a double-decker ice cream cone?
Or walked barefoot in the dewy morning grass?
Don't let life slip by
without relishing its simple pleasures.

Chapter
Four

Slowpokes

Life's
Too Short

to always take the fastest route the fastest route rather than the scenic one.

scenic one.

Life's
Too Short

to answer,
"How are you?"
with
"Busy."

slowpokes

Have you ever noticed that a young child is a natural slowpoke? Each activity becomes a world of its own, from getting dressed to building castles to eating breakfast. *Leisurely* is the preferred pace. No rushing. No demands. No pressure. *Hurry* is not listed in a young child's vocabulary.

Adults, however, hardly know how *not* to hurry. Rush to work, zip through projects, squeeze in lunch, run errands, and grab dinner at a drive-through. Whew! No wonder we're tired.

It's time to let the unhurried child of your past give you cause and help you pause for reflection. Time to take some deep breaths. Time to be the child who notices how many Cheerios are floating in a spoonful of milk. It's time to slow down.

Be still,
and know
that I am God.

PSALM 46:10

Life's
Too Short

to let "express lane"

describe your life.

to eat every meal in your car.

Life's
Too Short

in your car

Watch a snail in the moonlight.
Put together a thousand-piece puzzle.
Play and actually finish a game of Monopoly.
Build a house of cards. Daydream.
Recapture the joy of slow.

Chapter
Five

Comfort
Food

Life's Too Short to go to the fair and not eat cotton candy.

cotton candy

on top.

cherry on

to forget to put the

Life's
Too Short

comfort food

Comfort food. What images does that phrase conjure up in your mind? Creamy macaroni and cheese? Cinnamon toast? Homemade, chunky applesauce, still warm? Perhaps you recall chicken noodle soup served in a favorite mug or chocolate-chip cookies right out of the oven.

Whatever your comfort foods are today, they can probably be traced back to your childhood. In a society obsessed with low-carb foods and low-fat recipes, you may not readily divulge that you ate a hot-fudge sundae last night just because it reminded you of special times out with your mom.

Eating healthily is a good thing, but a helping of comfort food now and then can restore both body and spirit. So whether it's creamed tuna on toast or homemade chocolate pudding, whip up a batch and enjoy every bite.

Eat your food
with gladness.

ECCLESIASTES 9:7

Life's
Too Short

to drink hot chocolate without marshmallows.

Life's
Too Short

not to lick the
middle
out of an Oreo.

Treat yourself to your favorite comfort food.
No time to fix something homemade?
Buy a box of circus-animal crackers.
Curl up and eat them like a kid,
and you may just start feeling like one again!

Chapter Six

Further Adventures

Life's
Too Short

to panic over being lost—
enjoy the adventure.

Life's
Too Short
to leave
treasure hunting
to kids.

further adventures

Is this you? You drive the same route every day, work at a repetitive office job, and follow a basic routine at home. No wonder the child explorer in you is rarely satisfied.

Since it's unlikely you can set off tomorrow for the jungles of Africa, you may need to satisfy your thirst for adventure in other ways. Start mapping out your plans on paper by answering some questions. Where do you want to go? Not necessarily on a trip but in your life. What have you always wanted to do? What's keeping you from doing it?

Perhaps you lack the needed time or money. Or perhaps fear is blocking the way. If that's the case, maybe your dreams are exactly the new frontiers you need to explore and conquer. And when you do, your newfound courage is bound to lead you into even more of life's wonderful adventures.

Do not fear, for I am with you; do not be dismayed, for I am your God. I will strengthen you and help you; I will uphold you with my righteous right hand.

ISAIAH 41:10

Life's
Too Short

to be *afraid of walking*

a balance beam.

on a dark night.

a flashlight

to be bored with

Life's
Too Short

What adventure is beckoning you?
Don't let fear paralyze you.
Sign up for that class and learn mountain climbing,
public speaking, or scuba diving.
Or perhaps parachuting?
The sky's the limit!

Chapter Seven

Secret Hideout

Life's
Too Short

to give up dreaming of

never-never *land.*

Life's
Too Short
to always *color* inside the lines.

secret hideout

Remember your childhood secret hideout? You know, that cozy cranny where you could create your own imaginary world. A place that was yours and yours alone.

It may have been a tree house. Or maybe it was a magical room formed by branches that hung to the ground, creating a canopy of green where sunbeams and shadows danced. Perhaps your hideout was the snug shelter of a blanket fort where only you could fit.

Whatever it looked like, your special spot offered a place to daydream. A place to wander wherever your thoughts would take you. A place where your imagination could soar. The tree house became your castle in the forest, the blanket fort your cabin in the wilderness.

How long has it been since your imagination took flight? Since the impossible seemed possible? Maybe it's time you found a place to dream again.

God can do anything, you know—
far more than you could ever
imagine or guess or request in
your wildest dreams!
He does it . . .
by working within us.

EPHESIANS 3:20
THE MESSAGE

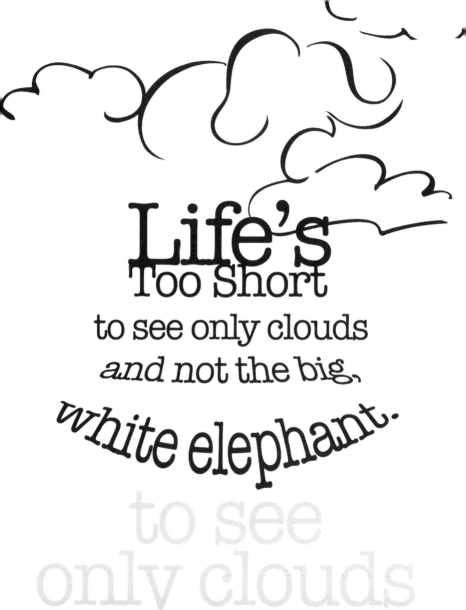

Life's
Too Short

to see only clouds
and not the big,

white elephant.

to see
only clouds

Life's
Too Short
to quit asking,
what if . . . ?

Find an enchanting spot
that gives your imagination wings.
Spend a little time dreaming.
Let God inspire you with His limitless
possibilities for your life.

Chapter
Eight

Holiday
Magic

Life's
Too Short

to stop sending

valentines to best friends.

Life's
Too Short

to open the door

to trick-or-treaters

without wearing

a mask.

holiday magic

Is there anything more magical for a kid than a holiday? Remember how your anticipation would grow like a big balloon filling with air? How your tummy would tingle with excitement? You couldn't wait to see your favorite cousins, play your favorite games, and eat your favorite foods. Holidays lifted life into the sublime. Colorful memories are probably etched in your mind so deeply that you can replay the scenes years later.

As an adult, major holidays are often associated with expense and effort. The minor ones are often ignored altogether. Yet every holiday shimmers with hope and joy for a child. If those special times have lost their luster for you, dust off your childlike spirit and make those days sparkle again.

Go home and prepare a feast,
holiday food and drink;
and share it with those
who don't have anything.

NEHEMIAH 8:10
THE MESSAGE

"Rudolph the Red-Nosed Reindeer"

Life's Too Short to sing "Rudolph the Red-Nosed Reindeer" and not add the silly parts.

Life's
Too Short

to eat
the fruitcake.

Hang a paper basket of May Day flowers on
the doorknob of a neighbor and run away in glee.
Wear green and a grin on St. Patrick's Day.
Sing Christmas carols with gusto!

Chapter Nine

Welcome Home

Life's
Too Short

to think

Sunday school
is just for kids.

Sunday school

...o sing "Jesus Loves the Little Children" and think it doesn't include you.

Life's
Too Short

welcome home

Is there a yearning within the deepest part of you? A longing that can't be satisfied? A restlessness?

Your child-heart is trying to find its home. A place of rest and peace. A place of true contentment, where your wandering soul will want to reside forever. That place is in the embrace of your heavenly Father.

God is love. Simple words that even a child can understand. Simple words we adults too often complicate. Yet the truth and beauty of those words remain as changeless as God Himself. He loves you. Yes, you. He always has and always will. You don't have to "wash up" or change a thing before coming to Him. He longs to welcome you just the way you are.

Listen to your Father's loving voice. He's saying, "Come home, My child. I've been waiting for you."

Unless you change
and become like little children,
you will never enter
the kingdom of heaven.

MATTHEW 18:3

Life's
Too Short

to equate childlike faith

with childish behavior.

Life's
Too Short

to forget
that

the Lord's Prayer
begins with "Our Father."

Allow the child in you
to run to your heavenly Father.
Jump into His arms for the biggest hug of your life.
And then let Him take you by the hand forever.